Deep Time
Black Bough Poetry

Edited by Matthew M. C. Smith

Guest Readers: Jack Bedell, Laura Wainwright, Ankh Spice

Illustrator: Rebecca Wainwright

Composer: Stuart Rawlinson

www.blackboughpoetry.com

Twitter: @blackboughpoems

FB: BlackBoughPoetry

First published by Black Bough Poetry in 2020.

Copyright © 2020.

LEGAL NOTICE

Matthew M C Smith has asserted his right under Section 77 of the Copyright, Designs and Patents Act 1988 to be identified as the editor of this work. Individual contributors reserve copyright to their work. Typesetting by Matthew M. C. Smith. Artwork by Rebecca Wainwright.

All rights reserved. No part of this book may be reproduced, stored in a retrieval system, or transmitted in any form, or by any means; electronic, mechanical, photocopying, without prior permission from the editor / authors. However, short extracts may be quoted on social media.

Inspired by, and dedicated to, Robert Macfarlane

*With thanks to the Black Bough poetry team
and all the artists involved*

'It is a common trope in underworld stories from across cultures and centuries that a small entrance-point opens into complex hidden space. *Underland* acted merely as that entrance-point for this *Black Bough* volume; the writers and artists gathered here have carried out their own fathomings and explorations, and the result is a collection of work that feels both contemporary and mythic, urgent and ancient. Strange voices for strange times sing out here.'

Robert Macfarlane

'This new issue of *Black Bough* offers the reader a host of treasures. From the witty, evocative and lyrical work of Estelle Price, through the vibrant, energetic and dramatic writing of Jane Lovell and Jenny Mitchell, to exciting new work by Robert Minhinnick, there are so many wonderful poems to discover here. It's great to see a new journal offering so much to literary culture in Wales. All hail *Black Bough!*'

Jonathan Edwards (Editor, Poetry Wales)

'*Black Bough Poetry's* first volume gets off to a great start with its 'Deep Time' issue inspired by Robert Macfarlane's work. The poems draw you into chasms, crevasses, caverns and open water - sometimes with tactile language that lets the natural world speak for itself and sometimes in ways that tap into the long history of myth and symbolism associated with these places. You'll enjoy Black Bough Poetry's subterranean journey.'

A.M. Juster   Translator, poet and critic

'*Black Bough Poetry* have tapped into a wide range of deep time mythologies with this compilation featuring the work of forty poets from around the world, all inspired by Robert Macfarlane's *Underland* (2019). Each poet mines landscapes, from initial descents in bone caves to journeys to the bottom of the deepest ocean. Accompanied with divine illustrations by Rebecca Wainwright, the poems are organized into five sections inscribed with passages from *Underland* in epigraph. All poets are, in a sense, oracles; the worlds that these prophetic poems inhabit are at once ancient, futuristic, and of our time. This project is ultimately a dive deep into histories and selves, where poets and readers, alike, explore journeys through darkness to brilliant cosmic light - a shared creative source.'

Kim Harvey   Editor, *Palette Poetry Journal*

Foreword

'When viewed in deep time, things come alive that seemed inert [...] The world becomes eerily various and vibrant again. Ice breathes. Rock has tides. Mountains ebb and flow. Stone pulses. We live on a restless Earth.' (Robert Macfarlane, *Underland*)

In 2019, an extraordinary book was published, *Underland*, by Robert Macfarlane, an English writer, climate activist and Professor of English Literature at Cambridge. In this work, Macfarlane reflects memorably on a range of subterranean journeys through catacombs, caving systems, burial chambers, deep storage locations and a time-travelling journey down into a glacier.

The expeditions, described in moving, vivid, poetic prose, reveal the multifarious ways in which humans have created, ventured into, and utilised underlands; how the symbolism of the underland permeates cultures and the ways in which ideas and imaginings are projected onto the ground deep below our feet. Macfarlane mines a range of deep spaces, plummeting into mythologies, histories and deep geological time. There is a haunting aspect to the work because in all of the adventures, the spectre of the 'Anthropocene' lurks – the environmental degradation of the present - and concerns for future generations. 'The Anthropocene' defines the period that we live in, where humans have altered the planet, its ecosystems, landscapes, oceans, air and subterranean, to such an extent that there is most likely to be irreparable, irreversible damage.

Creatively, this is fertile underground, of course. Writers and artists have mused on the significance of the underland and underworld for thousands of years. While editing this volume, I re-read *The Odyssey* and *The Aeneid* and was taken by these ancient writers to visit the mythic dead. When reading the hundreds of poems sent to this project, we were transported across time and different societies. This has been an experience that has revealed to us how many religions, cultures, writers and artists have been drawn to this symbolism. It makes the achievement of *Underland* all the more noteworthy given the breadth of this subject.

In *Deep Time: Volume 1*, we are led below ground and sea through chasms, crevasses, caverns and open water, to the deep. Several poems directly engage with the same locations in Macfarlane's work, while other writers reveal their own awe-inspiring journeys and 'descents'.

On behalf of the editorial team, illustrator, and composer, we would like to thank Robert Macfarlane for giving us his blessing to curate this work, and also to his publishers Hamish Hamilton Books and Penguin UK for allowing us to reproduce some quotations. We have all read 'Underland' a number of times and also read Robert Macfarlane's previous published work. This has been an adventure for us all.

I would like to particularly thank Laura Wainwright, Ankh Spice and Jack Bedell for their editorial expertise, enthusiasm, commitment and their stunning poems; also thanks to 'Annwn', or Rebecca Wainwright, an Architect who has produced incredible, original artwork for both editions; thanks also to Stuart Rawlinson, who has not only provided poems for the second volume but also three atmospheric 'Deep Time' musical pieces. We look forward to you reading Volumes 1 and 2 and hope you enjoy the experience as much as we did. If you have read *Underland*, we recommend that you explore Robert Macfarlane's back catalogue and also look out for all of the artists' work, too.

With warm wishes,

Matthew M. C. Smith

Editor – Black Bough Poetry
Swansea – June 2020.

Contents

Descent

Poem Found on a Cave Wall *Laura Wainwright*	1
Cueva de las Manos *Ian Richardson*	3
Drawn *Karen Hodgson Pryce*	4
Our Deep Time *Paul Brookes*	5
Chthonic Lands *Dai Fry*	5
Red Echoes *Matt Gilbert*	7
The Deepening *Stuart Rawlinson*	7
Deeper *Ryan Norman*	8
Faith *Mary Earnshaw*	8
To the Wind *A.A. Parr*	9
Swan Song in the Geissenklösterle Cave *Iris Anne Lewis*	9
Caving is not an optional activity *Estelle Price*	10
Down Here *Lori Bodner*	10
Red King *Matthew M.C. Smith*	11

Open Ocean

Open Ocean *Clarissa Aykroyd*	13
Last chance to settle *Ankh Spice*	14
Solastalgia *Ankh Spice*	14
Smoo Cave *Lynn Valentine*	15
South, as I Escape *Amantine Brodeur*	15
Kate Mulvaney at Marsh's Edge *Jack Bedell*	16
Kate Mulvaney Sings Along the Bank *Jack Bedell*	17
Kate Mulvaney Dreams of Breath *Jack Bedell*	18
Continental Shelf *Nick Kearney*	20
Perspective in a Hare's eye *Jane Lovell*	20

Deep Go Our Roots

Deep Go Our Roots *Dai Fry*	24
Imagining a Forest Made of Freedom *Jenny Mitchell*	24
Root Life *Mary C. Johansen*	25
Mysterious Passage *Brian Beatty*	25
At the Chasm's Edge *Merril D. Smith*	26
Yieldings *Ceinwen E. Cariad Haydon*	26
Mycorrhizae (German and English versions) *Pax Morrigan*	27

The Deep

Mining *E. A. Moody*	29

Pithead *Matthew M. C. Smith*	29
Copper Hill *M.S. Evans*	30
The Gold *Carrie Danaher Hoyt*	30
Wheal Fortune *Polly Oliver*	31
Lungs *Steven J. Burke*	31

Anthropocene

Your Heart Goes with Glaciers *Kari Flickinger*	33
Glacial body *Ankh Spice*	33
Boulby *Daniel Gustafsson*	34
Anthropocene *Nicola Heaney*	35
Magna Mater Mobilis *Pax Morrigan*	35
Crystal Cave *Michael Dickel*	36
Linville Caverns, Humpback Mountain *Carol Parris Krauss*	36
Geomyces destructans *Carol Parris Krauss*	37
Carbon Dating *Robert Frede Kenter*	37
New River *Devon Marsh*	38
Six *Devon Marsh*	38
Palimpsest *Devon Marsh*	39
Hailstones *Robert Minhinnick*	39
More hailstones *Robert Minhinnick*	40
After Man *Matthew M. C. Smith*	40

Appendix

Concrete poem version of 'Drawn' by Karen Hodgson Pryce.	41

Contributors section   42

Illustrations

All illustrations by 'Annwn' - Rebecca Wainwright:

Cover art: Man, Minotaur, Mithras	
Cueva de las Manos	2
Niaux Footprints	6
Red Man	11
Kate Mulvaney	18
Axis Mundi	23
Back cover – Annwn	

DESCENT

'Winter sun follows them down the passage and lights up the chamber. It is, they see, a charnel house […] The relics shine with calcite, and dusting some of the bones is red ochre powder.'

(Robert Macfarlane, *Underland*)

Poem found on a Cave Wall

Inspired by Cueva de las Manos

Drip   drip

        somewhere   behind
or ahead,   to my right   *no*   left,

        a disorientation

of sound – as sirens   are half-heard   in stacked traffic,
but no pulsing blue at the end of this tunnel, always lengthening…
I am unfazed, forging beyond cold, the blood-tang of ore, going

        deeper,

travelling further from shape and allegory, my cairn of chains,
into Hubble's hollow – its schorl-winged matter, its hydrogen halls and holes…
I am heading one way, anticipating
no ecstatic reunions, no dreamt welcome home, channelling
only the consolation,

        sure as quartz,

of knowing, that this route was – and will also be – theirs:
a communion of loves and shadows, of traced hands;
a last leaping torch beam swung on life's dark art.

Note: Cueva de las Manos (Cave of Hands) is situated in Río Pinturas, Patagonia. It takes its name from colourful stencilled outlines of prehistoric human hands that adorn the cave walls.

Laura Wainwright

Cueva de las Manos

After the ice age, after the fire;
five mass extinctions.
I reach to high-five handprints of burnt ochre,
silhouetted on stone.

A selfie; sharing the same space
with the unknown human;
both of us, reaching,
to record our being.

Epidermal ridges connect, distances kiss,
infinity shivers through the continuum
in pixellated prints. Your presence
and absence, felt across time.

Ian Richardson

Drawn

```
                              if you
                           take the foot
                            path, you
         will                              Follow
         pass                               the
         the              a beast          trail
         cave  —  deftly drawn man         of tree
         wall                              ash to
         art                            mine shaft —
          a                              on — until
                                         you see
                                         a spire,
                                         a skull
                         bone sign. Then on, to
                          when            steel
                          meets           cloud,
                          and             whales
                          are             lost
                           in             the
                         choked           sea
```

```
                                                                    If
                                                                   you
         far too gone you've .back turn – extending, wood acrid    arrive
                                                                    at
                                                                   an
```

Karen Hodgson Pryce

See appendix for concrete version of this poem

Our Deep Time

From summer to winter,
from brightness to loss,
follow the memory site of the dead.

Chasms gape, open mouthed,
clefts of wounds that do not heal;
rocks hold a dissonance.

There are no constellations
in these starless rivers:
black flow decided by fall.

Hear rush in the underland, carve
of space by water's progress;
it discovers as it sculpts.

Sometimes rock is parched
Leaves chambers of echo:
bones and burial gifts return.

Paul Brookes

Chthonic lands

Souls roam through a spirit underland,
Neolithic warriors weave their dreams.
Deserted, lost to cities of the heart
as star-dead rivers flow, thick into the black.

Gods were worshipped here,
secret ways all absent from maps.
Stone gardens, forgotten laments.
Under rock and wood henge,
no horizon or silver moon shines.

Here trees whisper without voice,
Hyphae carry stories and sustenance.

Underland, geology folds deep.
Listen to a sough of wind,
a caress of dark imaginations.

Dai Fry

Red Echoes

Shifting presence, unshaped,
spirits through rock;
the dancers stirred

by echoes and breath.
Red of earth, they quicken,
as depthless fluidities unleashed;

sleepers leap and
tears rise through granite
from the well of a pulsing duct.

Matt Gilbert

The Deepening

Vertigo, the deeper I go
through crust, mantle and core.

There are no metaphors in
these depths – no Hades,
just the thrumming
fullness of stone.

Seams of ore
transmit like cables,
humming magnetic fields,

untuned, unreceived.
I drill down, always deeper,
to ground myself.

Stuart Rawlinson

Deeper

The old tree above
takes deep breaths

inflating the cavern's
underland.

Heavy mists suffocate
the torch once illuminating

umbilical roots,
feeding the hungry maw

that swallowed souls
searching for peace
in the afterlife.

Ryan Norman

Faith

Water flows through malachite,
makes green of her feet
as she threads herself
through skin-tight passages,
head a finger's breadth
below the rock;
until, face feathered
by chill fresh air,
she steps into echoing space.
A glimmer of daylight falls
from above.
She stands alone, in awe,
raising a silent hymn
to the almighty goddess, Earth.

Note: Inspired by Mary's journey in Alan Garner's 1976 story, *The Stone Book,* from *The Stone Book Quartet*.

Mary Earnshaw

To the Wind

Along the Agawa rock face
we stood, aching backs open
to the August wind, frigid lake
writhing down below.

Inside the damp cavern,
our histories revealed themselves
as red powder on white rock bone.

Mishipeshu's roar rose up from the depths,
but that wind carried your whisper.

We are almost home;
in that place we have never been,
we are almost undone.

A.A. Parr

Swan Song in the Geissenklösterle Cave

His fingers hold the bone
of my wing, carve holes.

Firelight flickers around rock walls.
He brings me to his mouth, gently blows.

Breath on bone flows.
Melody flutes through the cave.

Mute no longer, I sing.

Iris Anne Lewis

Caving is not an optional activity

Brecon Beacons school trip c.1975

It is not as if I am alone.
I can hear the jagged breath of the helmeted girl
crammed beside me. It is not as if

I have already forgotten
how the rock looked, pock-marked, yellowy
like a face stamped by infection. It is not as if

I can't hear water's voice, a long way below my feet
singing like my mother, suggesting a way out,
a journey through stone to light. It is only

that for the elongated minute we must sit
with head torches off, dark falls into my open mouth
begins to strip me from the inside.

Estelle Price

Down Here

Down here
we tread drifting lines
> *in a stony gray throat*
> *pulped with moss*

hands and feet slip
into sunken cracks
> *we crouch on salt shaken stones*
> *drop into ancient lungs*

we press thumbs
into jagged veins of rocks
> *to feel the pulse*
> *of a thousand years*

Lori Bodner

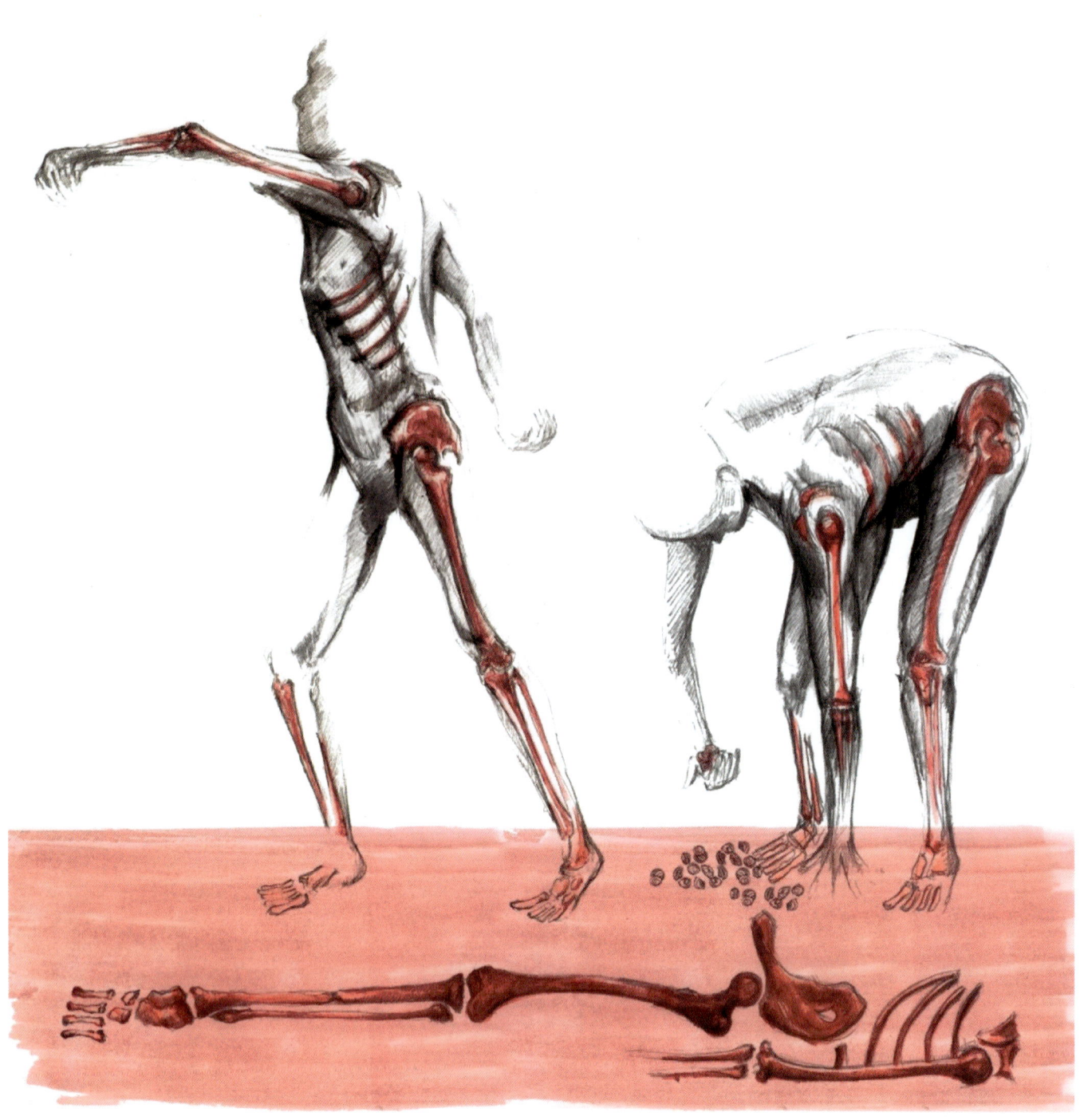

<u>Red King</u>

Royal sun rose;
rise, red king.

Matthew M. C. Smith

OPEN OCEAN

'Starless rivers run through classical culture, and they are the rivers of the dead. The Lethe, the Styx, the Phlegethon, the Cocytus and the Acheron flow from the upper world into the underland - and all five converge in a welter of water at the dark heart of Hades.'

(Robert Macfarlane, *Underland*)

Open Ocean

Royal BC Museum, Victoria, Canada

Endless drop
into darkness.
Through a window
in the sphere,
zones shade down
to the deepest hour,
the world's floor.

From the light, you can dream
of traces or beginnings,
but humankind
is written nowhere here.

Clarissa Aykroyd

Last chance to settle

On this long shard, we tiltwalk our builds and burials. Even low ground
here is eyrie, each rock the poke of sea-hid volcanoes – every scaffold

is a drowning. Squid-haunted rebar, whale-groaned cellars, ghostwater
of the Eocene – most of an island is a body trailing below a flood. Our small dry bones

are surface detail, the very oldest shallow-shook in hot iron sand, tapu
just seven scant centuries. The sea unsacreds us easily, all our smooths and roughs, our clingings on

to barely-unmolten peaks – wild teeth that cut bite early, fanging the bright thin air
above the sweet broad plate of Gondwanamama, easier geographies still unweaned. And we,

we hungry water-skimmers, we skeletons-in-waiting – left her alone
straining barely above the aching blue. When finally we landed

so late, so heavy
on this last unfooted earth, how she trembled,
how she held her breath.

Ankh Spice

Solastalgia

Half-done sun flares the water, light lancing clear depths
beneath an ape who swims these days for the joy of it
and a body's old map uncreases, reading happy accidents aloud

Tuck proud thumbs, and hands recall easy the flipper in the bone
and that they ruddered for a living, five million years gone

And below, a starling rush of rays murmurs round a mountain too sudden
for their species' long atlas, quaked up overnight, five thousand years gone

And above, a shoal of swifts, arrows shot true from their strings, zip the ghost-tree targets
of their hatching grove, felled overnight, five years gone

And that half-done sun is warm on anything like shoulders
for another 5 billion strokes or so, and the wind picks up cool now
and the clouds flickerframe – play at peaks and valleys, beasts and branches –
then wisp gone
and who doesn't love a blank, blue sky?

Ankh Spice

Smoo Cave

This is the place   where sea and river meet, where
a giant's mouth   was ripped   from the drop of the cliffs.
Inside we are hit with the soft slap of north,
a guide's broad accent,   the small stir   of the boat

A guddle of brown trout meet   and greet us,
tickling and dipping   at our outstretched hands.

We shelter from rain   where others once sat,

 stretch back to years   we can't count,

        lean in
           to ancient faces   reflected in our own.

Lynn Valentine

South, as I Escape

Fixed in its unsettling gaze, stone mouths breathe
through fissures, dark air whispers what's withheld
in the ceremonial climb. Bones of feet delve into
this muscular heartland; an azure archipelago lapped
circled by tides. Where stone memories hold traces
of tender extinction, tender collections of feet press
into intervals of absence, bare space; an eternity of
journeys vanished. Here, bones are but young in this
vertical breathing.

Amantine Brodeur

Kate Mulvaney at Marsh's Edge

> 'Just a few inches of soil is enough to keep startling secrets...'
> —Robert Macfarlane, *Underland*

All swamp fades into marsh eventually.
    Trees turn to ghosts, bushes
        give way to grass and then

open water. The old woman who taught
    Kate to heal showed her how
        to find this edge where

elderberry bushes and wild iris
    grew along the marsh grass.
        She knew the roots of these plants

dug all the way down into the broth
    of life and death sopping
        into everything under her swamp.

These roots, coaxed to surface,
make a bitter tea for the living.

Jack Bedell

Kate Mulvaney Sings Along the Bank

'to shelter what is precious, to yield what is valuable'
—Robert Macfarlane, *Underland*

At the new moon, she walks the water's edge
      each dawn singing a slow song
            into the crawfish holes sprung up

along the bank. From a boat on water
      you might think her song absent-minded
            and free. When the moon turns full, though,

she'll kneel at each hole mid-song,
      crack in two eggs letting the yolks
            sink down to the swamp's

    gullet. She'll stir mint into each tunnel
           and wait. If her notes hold true,
                the swamp will cough up

catfish after catfish from each hole,
a writhing bounty from its dead.

Jack Bedell

Kate Mulvaney Dreams of Breath

> 'We are often more tender to the dead than to the living,
> though it is the living who need our tenderness most.'
> —Robert Macfarlane, *Underland*

Since the day she stepped off the road into it,
    she has known how the swamp breathes.
        She's felt it expanding and releasing

under her feet, sunk down into it
    in her dreams, taken its water
        into her every hole and crevice.

The swamp's dead swim to her in these dreams,
    deep below its surface. She holds them like
        sunlight, sings away their pain.

For the living, she stews herbs and roots
    pulled from underneath the swamp
        to help them breathe, or stop all breath.

She knows there's no softer thing she can share
with the living, no greater gift from the dead.

Jack Bedell

Continental Shelf

My daughter kicks up leaf mould;
a blenny nosing along the riverbed.
The canopy threshes, dancing in clear air.

The understory, undisturbed
sways slow like a kelp forest, keeping its own time.
We slide through the dappled half-light of seedlings and moss
while thought slips deep down into the slow dark:
the pelagic ocean of mould and mycelia.

We drift near the surface,
careful,
aware of the abyss.

Nick Kearney

Perspective in a Hare's eye

Skyline erupts into tree, backlit and spilling
its own horizon across a perfect black moon,
an anti-matter moon brimming

deep pool silence: a world where nothing moves
till a thousand fathoms down, blunt and primeval,
they drift at you, curious at your veins fizzing,

your mouth yielding glassy planets of air.
Jaws champ, lamp-eyes drift back into blackness.
The moment holds you in its ocean.

This is the place where no one will find you:
no one sees you, except the hare, sudden
and skyswept, poised on a grassblade of decision.

Jane Lovell

Note: first published in *Bare Fiction Magazine.*

DEEP GO OUR ROOTS

'A deep time awareness might help us see ourselves as part of a web of gift, inheritance and legacy stretching over millions of years past'.

(Robert Macfarlane, *Underland*)

Deep Go Our Roots

An age progressed.
Not years of rock
but by a measure of forest,
beard of the earth.

This temperate land
rooted deep in seasons.
Summer burnt, wind whipped,
showered by rain.

Under sun and sister stars,
far-sighted leaf crown.
In a forest tangle,
the green man holds court.

Comet watcher,
below this weathered sky.

David Fry

Imagining a Forest Made of Freedom

They're bubbling, black roots reforming
pushing at the soil. Bones misshapen
with slave labour, straighten and grow strong,
ripping through the ground.
Fractures caused by beatings fuse, shape young trees
swelling to enormous trunks, fed with blood unjustly spilt.
Welts, deep-planted by a whip, design a hardy bark.
Starvation in reverse makes fertile leaves
wave, carefree at last.

Jenny Mitchell

Root Life

Existing unseen,
hidden below daylight
and weather,
sturdy networks
supply strength,
give sustenance,
anchoring for life.

Mary C. Johansen

Mysterious Passage

To hunt I hide
behind birch trees,
the forest's
lightning bones.

I find my way, like a circling hawk,
by following animal prints
through the snow.

There are doors in the wild
that only open

when I'm alone.

Brian Beatty

At the Chasm's Edge: Occulting

Dream or memory?
Ancestors call from this hollow land
pitted with strata of skeletal remains,
where smoke and ash snow-drifted to saturate the soil.

But at the chasm's edge
the roots of the maple tree
tunnel down, finding nourishment in a black hole—
endless, timeless, and potent--

in this abyss, it's fortified--
gilded branches rise,
drip dewdrop tears.

Merril D. Smith

Yieldings

Beneath my feet, earth
cradles kernels, growth
fed by minerals drawn
from rocks, laid down
aeons ago. Life's dance
emerges – flies on winds,
in water from aquifers and
warmth from our natal star.
Without our buried bedrock
all vital motion is in vain.

Ceinwen E. Cariad Haydon

Mycorrhizae

D Schwüm schwümmen ärdeschön im Härd
u tüpfe chrüselig verchnüpft d Haarwürzli
vomne mügerlige Grotzli aa.
Si spienzlen ihri Elemänt bim müntschele
u imene Momäntli drängt dr Fosfor mitm Schtickschtoff obsi,
Zuckerfau vom Himu nidsi.

Mycorrhizae

The fungi swim earthgorgeously in soil
and delicately bump ripple-intertwined the tiny root hairs
of an undernourished sapling.
Both showily display their elements while kissing
and in a short moment phosphorus and nitrogen urge upward,
sugarfall from the sky down.

Pax Morrigan

THE DEEP

'The oldest of underland stories concerns a hazardous descent into darkness in order to reach someone or something consigned to the realm of the dead'

(Robert Macfarlane, *Underland*)

Mining

Headlamp clicked into place,
I descend the pit, into the core,
towards the dark centre
at the heart of things.

Not just the story, the myths,
the talk of its heat.

Slowly, downwards, I touch
the channel's wall; beyond
the pool of lamplight,
wetness gathers
beneath my fingernails.

Is this the seam, the ripped mantle,
the place where truths are mined?

E. A. Moody

Pithead

The shafts of the underland shuttle, thunder,
din and dirge in fall to seam.

The pick and heave and crack of ore,
scraped, shovelled, into shunted carts.

Lamps light faces of lean musculature,
eyes level at shimmer of silica.

The underland erupts with hoisting of gear;
men cast out, spill from mouth

to kiss of sun in crown of valley,
a baptism cold in cool pit baths.

Dust streams through drains, yet lingers long
in chambers of flesh.

Matthew M. C. Smith

Copper Hill

A mile down,
tongueless throats
of tunnels gape.

Along walls, damp with sweat,
private offerings remain;
worn coins and glass beads.
Tokens of a sunlit world,
to help them find their way.

Atop the mountain's
dusty back, miners' shacks,
shoulder to shoulder;
a brotherhood of rough planks
and liquor's breath.

At night, we open
the cellar's hatch,
to let the shifts of spirits pass.

M.S. Evans

The Gold

took the lives
of those who dared descend
to pry its shiny death
from this rocky soil,
left miners in a darkness
still less pitch than that
which swallowed the souls
of living rich, damned
to deeper depths
by weight of it.

Carrie Danaher Hoyt

Wheal Fortune

Thin skin of heath and acid soil
stretched over metallic veinlets;
network of toxic treasures –
fortune for a few. Hewn out
by villagers lying quiet
beneath aligning church towers.

Under the blue arc of lark notes,
a portal crowned with gold ragwort.
Echoes ring here of playground warnings
of dropping dark fathoms, Alice-like,
to a realm of buccas, strange knockings
and lost ghosts.

Polly Oliver

Lungs

Below my childhood home, fifty fathoms down,
tunnels were hewn by naked sweating men
who mined black gold for bread, for rent.

They bore into danger, found fossilised forest;
it spat slack as they broke it free, breathing
the dust of prehistory, sealing untimely deaths.

Steven J. Burke

ANTHROPOCENE

'The crevasses glow a version of the unearthly blue we saw on Apusiajik. Here the blue is even more intense, more radiant, older'

(Robert Macfarlane, *Underland*)

Your Heart Goes with Glaciers

Like liquid, the mind overextends. Bygone water yawns
blue. Twelve billion tons gush below the connect, deep
into a convex hollow—a glacial melt. Manipulate time
to watch our arms end. Lacuna. A river guide—
remember the way that water flows around
frowning holes, track the speed of water in forgotten lips. Think—
if you dropped an absent leaf, all of autumn would be swallowed. Leveled.
No time for wave motions or breath. Every lover slips down that stream. Watch.
See loose clouds, lightning, aperture wheels in greasy sky. Hear
dysphonic wails of cellos, the slice of nails over the flesh of drums. Our
symphony of collision. Your eyes, your hands melt glaciers. Your fingertips
sever from this plundered epoch. Wave your softness to cut a shore.

Kari Flickinger

Glacial body

Under magnification, human bone alive
is skimmed aurora, and the fracture a cliff
of wind-cut ice. To snap up the blue hum
of a glacier, the human eye crackles focus
and there we lie, glow laid bare to the aeon-blade
flensed of our cushion dirt. The owner of this bone
will survive the moraine, fallen deep
to the chill dark of chemical sleep, while the rill of his pulse
quivers that brutal cliff and complicates the fix
and in the dark the ice too is moving to the wiles
of its own slow will, vitals steady.
We think it unconscious. We think it dead.
They say I am lucky to shiver awake, but luck would mean forgetting
old bones have no colour at all – lost airless, pressed lightless.

Ankh Spice

Boulby

I

The need for gods
        beneath us now,
we mine moor and seabed,

bore the bedrock
        with bloodshot eyes,
burrow, scrut and scry.

II

Sifting sandstone,
           silt and halite,
straining dust for stars,

to catch a light-
           eluding prey,
we tunnel time itself.

III

Where truth leaves us
        trailing shadows,
questions cave to prayer,

probe the haloed
           heart of matter,
delve the answering dark.

Daniel Gustafsson

Anthropocene

Undulating with the tides
a seventh continent floats
in the navy reaches of the Pacific.

Whipped by winds and ocean eddies
still the fluid footprint floats,
a wasteland of microplastics.

In the city, an empty bottle
floats in the gutter. A seagull swoops
overhead, its reflection dancing
across the mawkish puddle.

Nicola Heaney

Magna Mater Mobilis

My father told me of the grave mound on the hill, webbed in roots
of lichened beeches, sky-tall firs. Three-thousand-year-old quiet dark,
dispelled, revealed faint mineral shadows cast on soil, the bones
acid-trickled long ago away into the ground.
More lasting was a bracelet teased and polished of sapropelite:
pressed living rock from when the mountains were still sea
conserving in their breathless depth uncycled death
before the land rose. And great glaciers hewed the latitude, cast
aside the debris of their toil, piled high the hill on which the mound
was built before the forest grew. Soon, there will be a gravel pit.
Old treasure once more tapped for dwellings and for gravel paths
with stones unstacked. And father will tell my niblings of the mound
where no hill is, and no trees are, while their small hands fill playfully
with pebbles from old Tethys Ocean washed with liquid bones.

Pax Morrigan

Crystal Cave

In Western Wisconsin, not far
from land that glaciers missed,
signs invite you into the Crystal
Cave. Karst towers and sinkholes
dramatize the open mouth yawning
in front of you. The dark waits,
weaving among glimmering lances,
stalactites and stalagmites—
water drops and quartz glints—
the ever-changing paths
of wet stone end where
crystals reflect ineffable
futures that glaciers miss.

Michael Dickel

Linville Caverns, Humpback Mountain

Mountain collapsed, a bindle full of woes
and weary strapped to his back, affixed

by lichen and laurel. Mountain lamented
limestone tears, coursed underland

streams - only the blind trout to witness.
Mountain died, spine slumped, bones

arched, ribbed vaults. A body emptied, a cave
cathedral - scriptures of the dark world carved

on the walls; a dirge sung by bats.

Carol Parris Krauss

Geomyces destructans

Old Man Rufus said the blind trout are gone,
nibbled up by rabid river otters, and the bats
have contracted the lesion disease, dropped
dead on the new concrete pathway.

You can purchase a two-for-one Groupon
to tour the caves. Artificial lights guide you.
No-one will stumble in the dark, with all this
in place to illuminate our future.

Carol Parris Krauss

Carbon Dating

Ice rising up to chip and chisel.
Haunted hands full, arm loads—the dead trees,
split decades ago—to burn.
The storm calls, sky bears down.
Otter songs, wild honey, a heron lands lakeside.
Generations of ashes carved away, and the old
men and women buried uphill, the child's grave—
imperceptible as deer tongues threading red fungus
in four-four rhythm. I want to be burned here, too,
with the three hundred year old trees—
a secret cove of driftwood, boxes
of cracked tubes—generations of radio listeners.
Now million dollar houses come with skis, prop planes, gardens,
and we bottle the ice, burn the woods, freezing inside,
not daring to talk about what we torched, choking the sun.

Robert Frede Kenter

New River

The New wends north bearing a misleading name;
only three other rivers follow an older course.

On a railbed trail, children on bicycles marvel
at a geologic rainbow, pink phlox, a black snake.

My family rides through morning to a picnic,
afternoon to wade in the river, after dinner to lie

in a field and ponder the zodiac. Fireflies
rise to constellate the air. Riffles offer

a song older than starlight: water motivating
abrasion, thinking of the sea. Nothing thinks of me,

my kin oblivious, consumed in a singularity—
this moment suspended above the depth of time.

Through us, the universe reflects. Out there
infinity; in dew-wet grass, its wondrous other half.

Devon Marsh

Six

Our frozen cores hold mammoth breaths
for millennia in sintered snow. Our base
may be our undoing, so write my story
in graphite. Let it say hiraeth at night.

My descendants will follow concrete paths
to seek a trace of me, though signs lie
all about. When we go out, our extinction
will be sealed beneath a thin plastic line.

I would rather my distant heirs know my
own wonders: grazing deer, the Milky Way,
cool air. Nocturnal calls of whippoorwills
drifting through an open bedroom window.

Devon Marsh

Palimpsest

Past Oconee bridge, a gravel road
led to a fish camp washed away by flood.

My grandfather designed its lodge
on Lucky Strike posters from his store.

Digging footings by hand, he found the pink
chert projectile point that rests on my desk.

On her only visit, washing diapers
from a johnboat's stern, my grandmother felt

the current take hold. She bloodied her hands
pulling back to shore by a rusted chain.

At their graves I hear cicadas, mowers,
her voice naming churches drowned by the lake.

Devon Marsh

Hailstones

Hail in my hair,
sharp as the stars
of Aquarius…

Robert Minhinnick

More hailstones

A spasm of hail.
In the gutters it smokes as it vanishes.
This creature is becoming a negative of itself.
Chalk around a corpse.

Robert Minhinnick

After Man

The fern, the ivy,
the circle of oaks,
were fast losing names given;
they obeyed no other law
than the rise and retreat
of season and star.

With creep of sap,
decay and renewal,
our time was terribly mocked.

Matthew M. C. Smith

Appendix

The concrete version of Karen Hodgson Pryce's poem, 'Drawn':

Drawn

If you take the foot path,
you will pass the cave wall art –
a deftly drawn man, a beast

Follow the trail of tree ash
to mine shaft – on – until you see
a spire, a skull bone sign.

Then on, to when steel
meets cloud, and whales
are lost in the choked sea.

If you arrive
at an acrid wood, extending –

turn back.
you've gone too far

Karen Hodgson Pryce

Contributors

Artist

Rebecca Wainwright is an Architect living and working in London. Her art focuses on exploring the relationship between natural and built forms and bridges fine art, sculpture and digital art. Twitter: @wainwrightrebs rebeccawainwrightart.com

Composer

Stuart Rawlinson is a British poet and composer based in Brisbane. His poems have appeared in various publications and his debut collection, *Encyclopaedia of Trees*, was published in 2013. He maintains a literary blog at stuartrawlinson.com Twitter: @mrsturawlinson

Contributors

Laura Wainwright is from Newport, South Wales. Her poems have been published, and are forthcoming, in a range of magazines, journals and anthologies. She was shortlisted in the Bridport Prize poetry competition in 2013 and 2019, and awarded a Literature Wales Writer's bursary in 2020 to finish writing her first poetry collection. She is also author of the book, *New Territories in Modernism: Anglophone Welsh Writing 1930-1949* (University of Wales Press, 2018).

Ian Richardson is a Scottish writer. Overall winner in Scottish Borders 'Waverley Lines' September 2015, Ian was also presented with the Anstruther Writing Award in November 2016. Since 2018, he has studied haiku and micro-poetry, examples of which can be found on Twitter: @IanRich10562022

Karen Hodgson Pryce lives in Aviemore, Scotland. Her poetry is found in *Northwords Now*, *Butcher's Dog*, *Black Bough Poetry (Winter 2019)*, *Lighthouse (Issue 21)*, *The Poets' Republic* and *Ink, Sweat & Tears*. She won 3rd Prize in Café Writers Open Poetry Competition 2019.

Paul Brookes is a shop asst. who lives in Wombwell. His recent chapbooks include *Please Take Change* (Cyberwit.net, 2018), *Stubborn Sod* (Alien Buddha Press, 2019) and *As Folk Over Yonder* (Afterworld Books, 2019). Forthcoming is *Our Ghost Holiday*. He edits *The Wombwell Rainbow Interviews*. Twitter: PaulDragonwolf1 FB: PaulBrookesWriter www.thewombwellrainbow.com/

Dai Fry is a poet living on the south coast of England. He is originally from Swansea, and Wales remains a huge influence on everything in his life. His work has been published in *Black Bough poetry*, *The Hellebore Press* and *Re-Side*. He is a regular contributor to #TopTweetTuesday.
Twitter: thnargg@me.com www.seekingthedarklight.co.uk

Matt Gilbert is a poetry-dabbling, place-pondering, musically promiscuous, book-loving copywriter. Originally from Bristol, he now lives in South London and regularly blogs at richlyevocative.net Twitter: @richlyevocative

Ryan Norman is a writer from New York living in the Hudson Valley. Inspired by the landscape, he writes what he feels. His poetry often interweaves mental health, mythology, and nature. You can find his past work in *Elephants Never*, *3 Moon Magazine*, and *Storgy Magazine*. Twitter: @RyanMGNorman

A. A. Parr is a Canadian writer, artist and entrepreneur with a Spec Honours BFA from York University. She writes a weekly series of poetry for strangers on Channillo.com @_Channillo and her debut chapbook, *What Lasts Beyond the Burning*, is forthcoming from Nightingale & Sparrow Press @nightandsparrow in 2020. Twitter: @ifitfeelswrite

Mary Earnshaw's writings have, over the last few years, become shorter and shorter – and sometimes don't happen at all. She writes what she sees (and hears, smells, feels, imagines) on her paths through life, which sometimes end in cul-de-sacs. Her poetry is published in *Broken Spine* and *Visual Verse*. Twitter: @MaryEarnshaw

Iris Anne Lewis writes poetry and short stories. Her work has featured at the Cheltenham Literary Festival and the Bradford on Avon Arts Festival. She has been successful in competitions and is published in magazines and anthologies. Twitter: @IrisAnneLewis

Estelle Price is a poet from Cheshire who has been shortlisted in many competitions including the Bridport, Yorkmix, Wells and Welshpool. She was long listed for the 2019 National Poetry Competition. Estelle writes wherever she finds herself and has long been afraid of the dark. Twitter: @EstelleHPrice

Lori Bodner is a published travel writer, poet, and adventurer of far-flung places. A nature seeker and eternal trekker, she writes best with her dog nearby, indoors or out. Twitter: @yogamogaflow

Clarissa Aykroyd grew up in Victoria, Canada and now lives in London. Her debut pamphlet is *Island of Towers* (Broken Sleep Books, 2019). Her poems have appeared in publications including *The Interpreter's House*, *Lighthouse*, *The Island Review* and *Strange Horizons*. Twitter: @stoneandthestar
www.thestoneandthestar.blogspot.co.uk

Ankh Spice is a sea-obsessed poet from Aotearoa (NZ). His poetry has appeared in a wide range of international publications and has twice been nominated for the Pushcart Prize. He truly believes that words have the power to change the place we're in, and you'll find him doing his best to prove it on Twitter: @SeaGoatScreams or on Facebook: @AnkhSpiceSeaGoatScreamsPoetry

Lynn Valentine writes between dog walks on the Black Isle. Her work has been widely published online and in print anthologies. She is currently organising her first poetry collection under the mentorship of Cinnamon Press after winning a place on the Cinnamon Pencil competition.

Forthcoming from Amantine Brodeur during 2020 is 'Beneath the Waters of Liars' in *Pink Plastic House Journal* this summer and *'In The Scattering of Tongues'*, an exploration of Beckett's women, in the winter issue of *Thrice*. Twitter: @AmantineB

Jack B. Bedell is Professor of English and Coordinator of Creative Writing at Southeastern Louisiana University where he also edits *Louisiana Literature* and directs the Louisiana Literature Press. Jack's work has appeared in *Southern Review, Birmingham Poetry Review, Pidgeonholes, The Shore, Cotton Xenomorph, Okay Donkey, EcoTheo, The Hopper, Terrain, saltfront*, and other journals. His latest collection is *No Brother, This Storm* (Mercer University Press, 2018). He served as Louisiana Poet Laureate 2017-2019.

Nick Kearney lived for 25 years in Valencia, Spain, where he published the children's story collections *Batiscafo en el Mar*, and *Batiscafo en las Nubes*. Now in Somerset, he has been writing poetry since childhood, but is largely unpublished, bar a poem in *OM Yoga Magazine*.

Jane Lovell's latest collection is *This Tilting Earth* published by Seren. She also writes for *Dark Mountain* and *Elementum Journal*. Jane is Writer-in-Residence at Rye Harbour Nature Reserve. FB: jane.lovell.3760
https://janelovellpoetry.wordpress.com/

Jenny Mitchell is joint winner of the Geoff Stevens' Memorial Poetry Prize (Indigo Dreams). She's published in *The Rialto, The Interpreter's House, Under the Radar* and others, etc. A debut collection, *Her Lost Language*, is published by Indigo Dreams.

Mary C. Johansen is a poet and writer living on Long Island, New York. Mary is also a photographer and avid yoga student. Twitter: @MaryCJohansen

Brian Beatty has published four collections of poetry: *Borrowed Trouble, Dust and Stars: Miniatures* (Cholla Needles Press, 2019 and 2018), *Brazil, Indiana* (Kelsay Books, 2017) and *Coyotes I Couldn't See* (Red Bird Chapbooks, 2016). He lives in Saint Paul, Minnesota.

Merril D. Smith is a historian and poet who follows rivers into the past and puts dreams into words. Sometimes the words get published. Twitter: @merril_mds Instagram: mdsmithnj
Blog: merrildsmith@wordpress.com

Ceinwen E. Cariad Haydon writes short stories and poetry. She is widely published in online magazines and in print anthologies. She is a Pushcart Prize and Forward Prize nominee and has an MA in Creative Writing from Newcastle University, UK (2017). She believes everyone's voice counts. Twitter: @CeinwenHaydon

Pax Morrigan is on a quest for imagination and loves playing with words. *Twitter*: @paxmorrigan
https://www.paxmorrigan.com

E. A. Moody has a PhD in Masculinity in Welsh writing and works in education in South Wales. This is Elizabeth's first poetry publication.

Matthew M. C. Smith is a writer from Swansea. He is published in *Icefloe Press, Barren Magazine, Other Terrain, Back Story* and *Broken Spine*. His first collection is *Origin: 21 Poems*. He is editor of Black Bough Poetry. Twitter: @MatthewMCSmith FB: MattMCSmith

M.S. Evans is a writer and visual artist. Originally from Seattle, she currently lives in Butte, Montana. Twitter: @SeaNettleInk Instagram: @permacrust

Carrie Danaher Hoyt is a poet/lawyer/mother/wife/person living outside of Boston. She has poems in several online journals, one spectacular blog and two printed anthologies. Carrie's poems have received Pushcart Prize & Best of Net nominations. Find her on Twitter: @CDanaherH

Polly Oliver hails from Cornwall and lives in Swansea. She's been writing poetry on and off for years, mainly reading it at open mic nights across the city and enjoys hearing the work of other local poets and spoken word artists. Her poems have been published in *Black Bough, Spillwords* and on her blog 'RocksandBones – Poems from the Celtic Fringes'.

Steven J Burke is an historian and history lecturer on the verge of completing a tortuous PhD thesis. He runs, walks and takes photographs. He also writes a bit of poetry, mostly about landscape, environment, nature, travel and mental health. Twitter: @Steven_J_Burke

Kari Flickinger's poems have been nominated for Best of the Net. She is an alumna of UC Berkeley and the Community of Writers. When she is not writing, she can be found singing to her large Highlander cat, Bear. Find her: Twitter: @kariflickinger www.kariflickinger.com

Daniel Gustafsson is a poet with an interest in northern landscapes and alliterative verse. He made his double debut in 2016 with *Alyosha* (Augur Press) in English and *Karve* (Axplock) in Swedish. Daniel's new pamphlet, *Fordings*, is out now from Marble Poetry. He lives in York. Twitter: @PoetGustafsson

Nicola Heaney is a Derry-born, Bristol-based poet. Her work has been shortlisted for the Bridport Prize and appeared in publications such as *The North* magazine, *Honest Ulsterman* and *Riggwelter*.

Michael Dickel grew up in the US Midwest and currently lives, writes, and teaches in Jerusalem, Israel. He used to live near the Crystal Cave that inspired his poem in this edition and currently lives near the Stalactite Cave, which he visits once in a while. His prize-winning poetry collection, *Nothing Remembers* (@FLPress), came out in 2019. Twitter: @MYDekel469 https://MichaelDickel.info

Carol Parris Krauss is a watcher and a digger. Her work can be located online and in print journals such as Amsterdam Quarterly and the SC Review.

Robert Frede Kenter is an author, visual artist, and EIC/publisher of *Ice Floe Press*. He has work recently published in *The Failure Bailer, Twist in Time, Anthropocene, Burning House Press, Cough* and others. A new chapbook hybrid, *Audacity of Form* (2019) is published by Ice Floe Press. Twitter: @frede_kenter

Devon Marsh served as a U.S. naval aviator before working for Wells Fargo Bank. His poetry has appeared in *The Lake, Poydras Review, The Timberline Review, Muddy River Review, Penmen Review, Loch Raven Review, The Kakalak Anthology of Carolina Poets*, and at http://devonmarsh.com Twitter: @DevonMarsh1

Robert Minhinnick is a Welsh poet, novelist, short story writer and essayist. He has won the Forward Prize twice, along with Wales Book of the Year a record three times – most recently for his poetry collection, *Diary of the Last Man* (Carcanet, 2017). *Diary of the Last Man* was also shortlisted for the T.S. Eliot Prize and has been made into a film, directed by Eamon Bourke. He is former editor of *Poetry Wales* and cofounder of Friends of the Earth Cymru and Sustainable Wales.

Printed in Poland
by Amazon Fulfillment
Poland Sp. z o.o., Wrocław